Body Systems

The Digestive System

J
61.2
.3

What makes me burp?

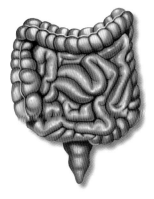

Sue Barraclough

Heinemann LIBRARY

www.heinemann.co.uk/library
Visit our website to find out more information about Heinemann Library books.

To order:
☎ Phone 44 (0) 1865 888066
🗎 Send a fax to 44 (0) 1865 314091
💻 Visit the Heinemann Bookshop at www.heinemann.co.uk/library to browse our catalogue and order online.

First published in Great Britain by Heinemann Library, Halley Court, Jordan Hill, Oxford OX2 8EJ, part of Pearson Education. Heinemann is a registered trademark of Pearson Education Ltd.

© Pearson Education Ltd 2008
The moral right of the proprietor has been asserted.

Editorial: Sian Smith, Cassie Mayer and Rebecca Rissman
Design: Debbie Oatley and Steve Mead
Picture research: Hannah Taylor and Maria Joannou
Production: Duncan Gilbert

Printed and bound in China by South China Printing Co. Ltd.

ISBN 978 0 431 13813 8

12 11 10 09 08
10 9 8 7 6 5 4 3 2 1

British Library Cataloguing in Publication Data

Barraclough, Sue
    The digestive system : what makes me burp? - (Body systems)
    1. Digestion - Juvenile literature 2. Digestive organs - Juvenile literature 3. Nutrition - Juvenile literature
    I. Title
    612.3

A full catalogue record for this book is available from the British Library.

Acknowledgements
The publishers would like to thank the following for permission to reproduce photographs: ©2008 Jupiterimages Corporation p.**10**; ©Alamy Images pp.**25**, **6** (Photofusion Picture Library); ©Corbis pp.**8** (Newmann, Zefa), **22** (Simon D. Warren, Zefa); ©Getty Images pp.**4** (Alexander Hassenstein, Bongarts), **28** (DK Stock), **12** (Nick Veasy), **7, 21** (Photographers Choice); ©Masterfile p.**5**; ©Rex Features p.**26** (Burger/ Phanie); ©Science Photo Library pp.**14** (Alfred Pasieka), **18** (David M. Martin MD), **16** (Susumu Nishinaga)

Cover photograph reproduced with permission of ©Punchstock (Stockbyte).

Every effort has been made to contact copyright holders of any material reproduced in this book. Any omissions will be rectified in subsequent printings if notice is given to the publishers.

Contents

Some words are shown in bold, **like this**. You can find out what they mean by looking in the glossary.

Why do I eat and drink?

You need food and water to stay alive and healthy. You need the **energy** from your food to move, breathe, and think. You also need energy to keep you warm and to grow. Water is needed for your body to work properly.

← Bananas are a good food for energy.

Everything you eat and drink travels through the digestive system in your body. This system breaks food into small pieces. The food can then be used by your body.

How is food used?

Lots of the food you eat is broken down into tiny parts called **nutrients**. Nutrients are carried to all of your body parts in your blood. **Glucose** is a nutrient your body uses to give you **energy**.

Fruit gives you vitamins which are important nutrients.

⬆ **Milk provides nutrients which are good for healthy bones and teeth.**

Your body uses nutrients to keep your skin and bones healthy. It also uses nutrients to mend your body. You need nutrients to stay healthy.

What is the digestive system?

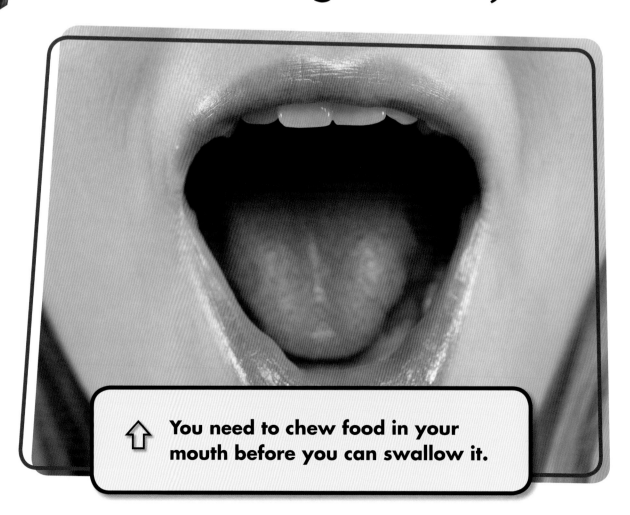

⬆ You need to chew food in your mouth before you can swallow it.

Digesting means breaking down food so that your body can use it. Many parts of your body help you to digest food. There are parts you can see, such as your mouth, tongue, and teeth.

There are also parts inside your body that you cannot see, such as your **stomach** and liver. These and other parts make up the digestive system.

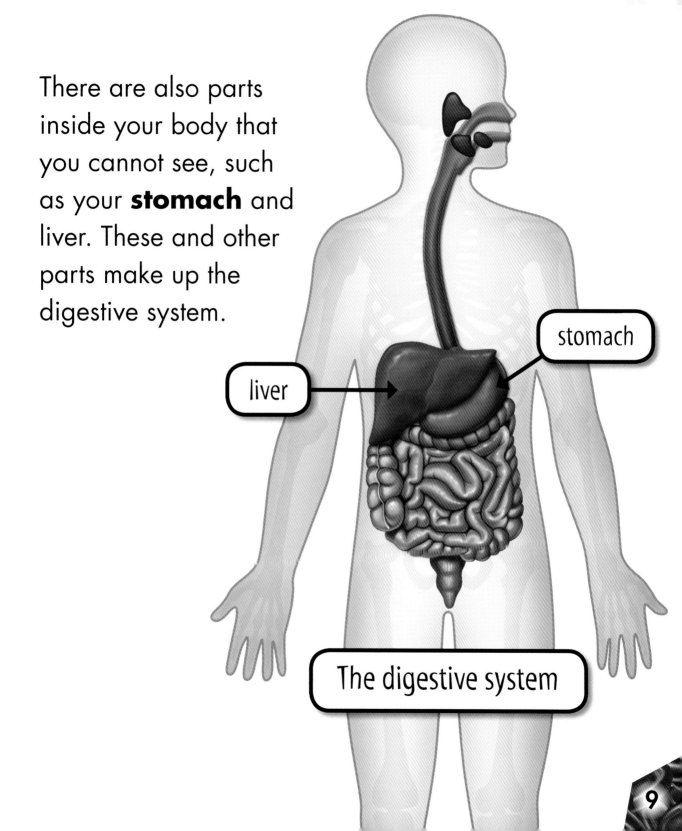

liver

stomach

The digestive system

What does my mouth do?

The different parts of your mouth crush and move your food. Your teeth cut and grind food. Your tongue pushes food around your mouth.

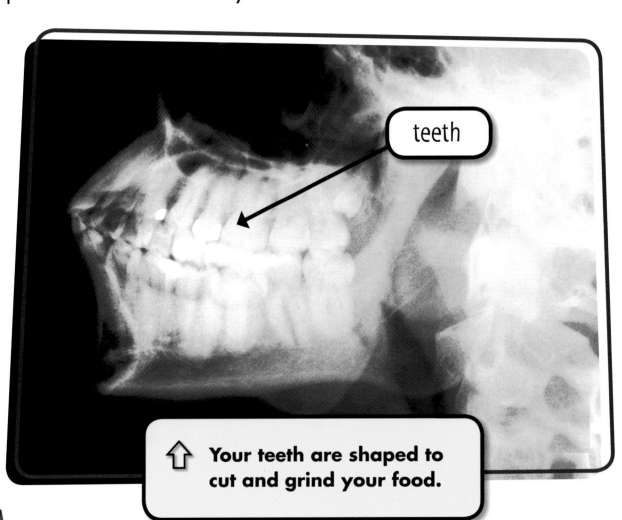

teeth

⬆ **Your teeth are shaped to cut and grind your food.**

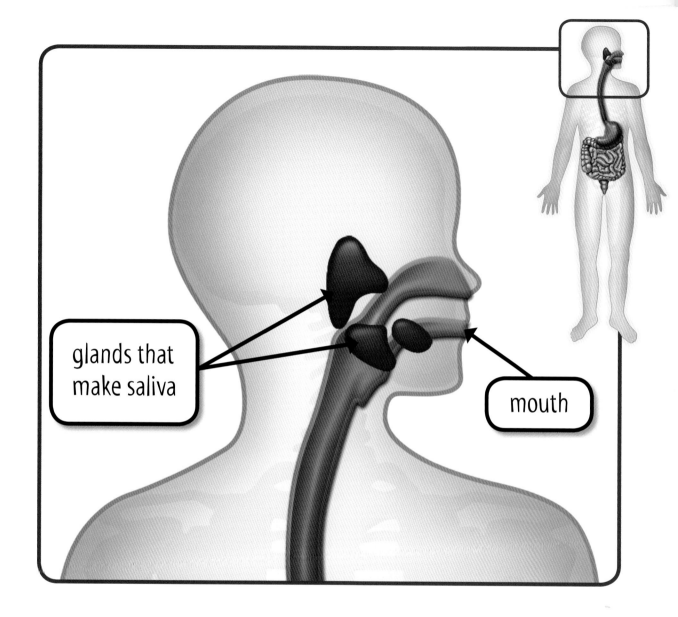

glands that make saliva

mouth

Saliva or spit is made in the mouth by **glands**. These glands make **enzymes** for your body to use. Enzymes in your digestive system help to break food down. Saliva is also mixed with food to make it soft and slippery. This makes it easier to swallow.

How do I swallow?

When food has been chewed it is ready to be swallowed. Your tongue pushes food to the back of your mouth. It is then pushed down your throat.

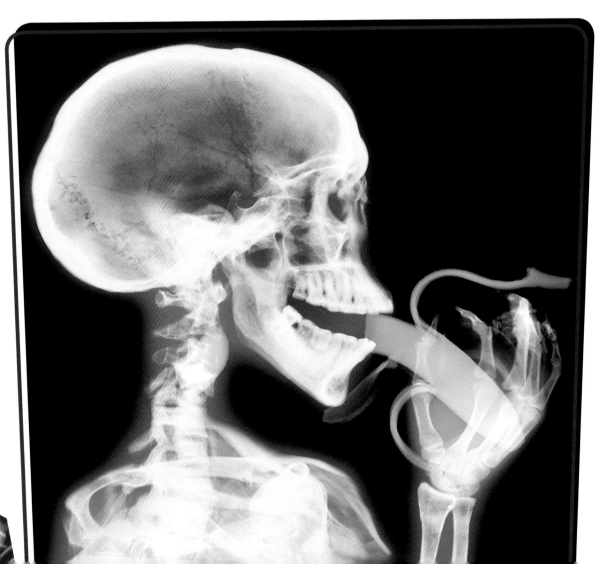

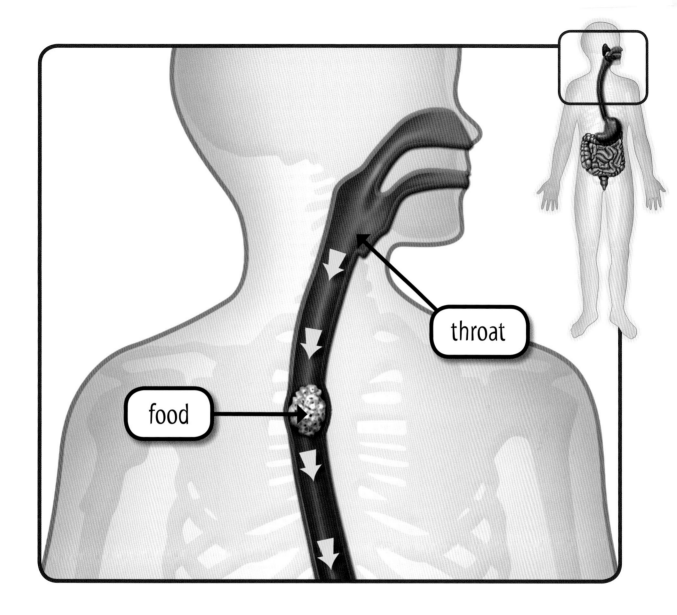

food

throat

The throat is a long tube that connects your mouth to your **stomach**. The **muscles** in the throat squeeze to push the food along. So you can swallow even if you are standing on your head.

What is my stomach?

Food travels quickly down the throat into the **stomach**. The stomach is a stretchy bag of **muscle**. It gets bigger when it is full of food and smaller when it is empty.

This picture was made using a computer. It shows the shape of the stomach inside your body.

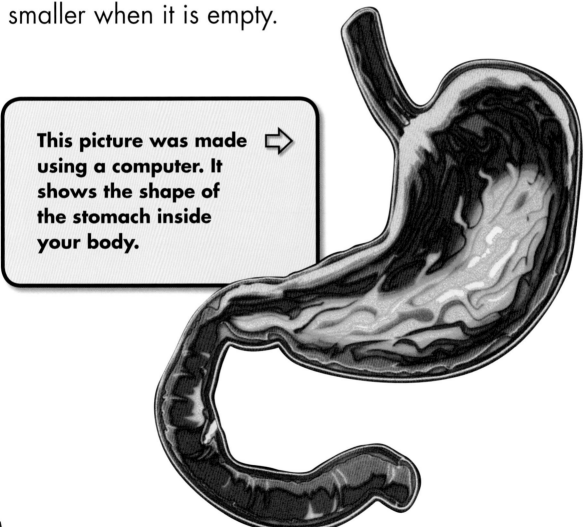

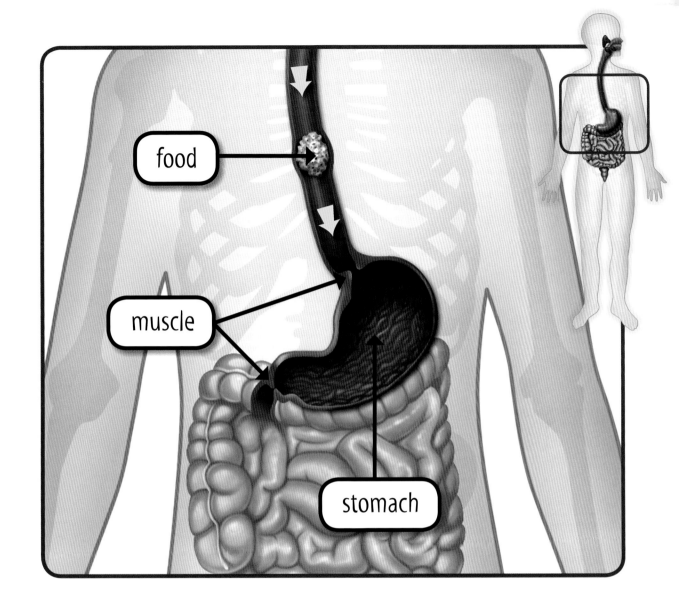

food

muscle

stomach

Your stomach is made of strong muscles. These muscles squeeze and move food in the stomach. There is also a ring of muscle at the end of the stomach that keeps food in.

What does my stomach do?

⬆ **This picture shows the inside of the stomach.**

It takes about four hours for food to move through your **stomach**. Food is mixed with **digestive juices** which are made by **glands** in your body. Digestive juices are full of **enzymes** which help to break down the food in your body.

The **muscles** in the wall of your stomach squeeze and mix food to break it down. When food is soft and **liquid**, the ring of muscle opens. This lets the liquid food out of the stomach.

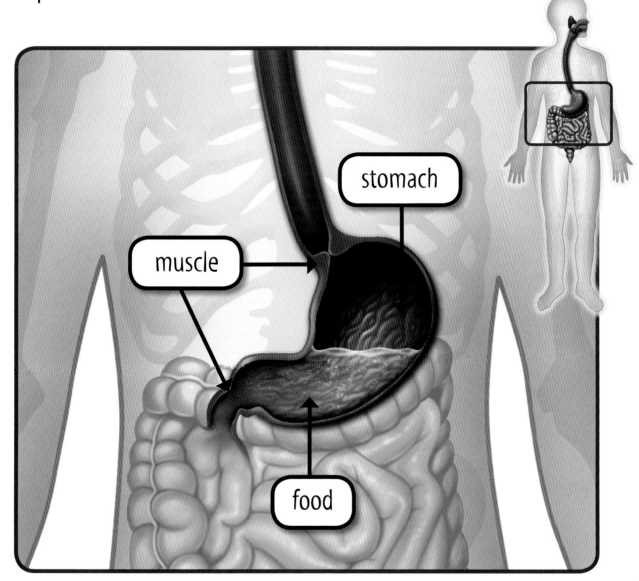

muscle

stomach

food

What is my small intestine?

Your small intestine is a tube that is very long and thin. **Liquid** food goes from the **stomach** into the small intestine. The liquid food is broken down into even smaller pieces in the small intestine.

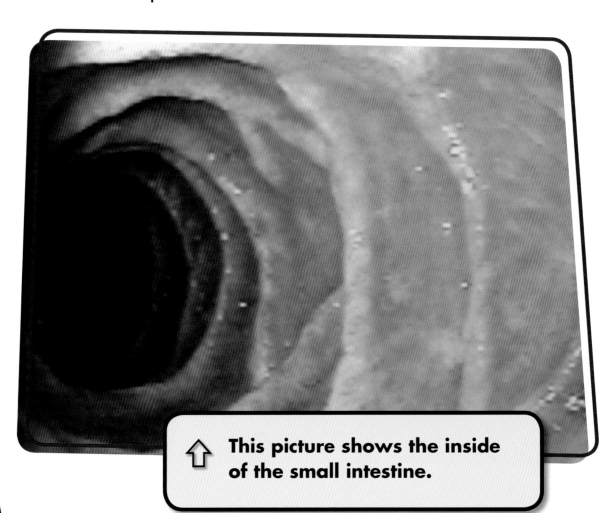

⬆ **This picture shows the inside of the small intestine.**

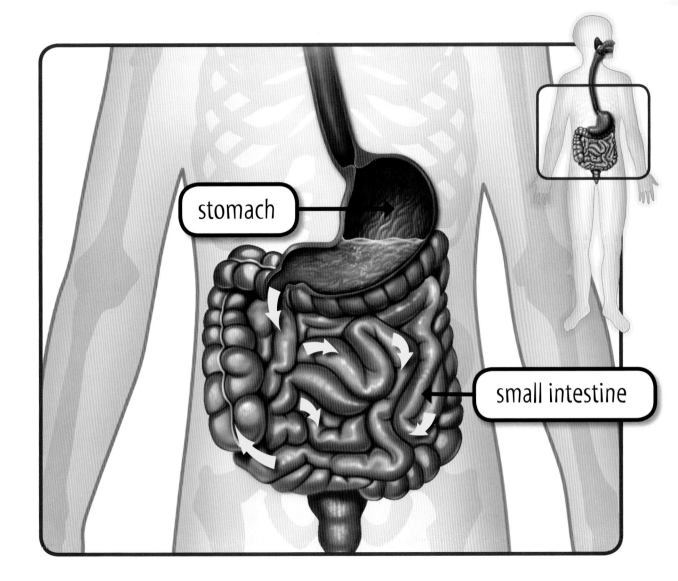

stomach

small intestine

Your food is broken down into tiny pieces called **nutrients**. The nutrients pass from the small intestine into your blood. Your blood carries the nutrients to every part of your body. Anything your body cannot use passes into the large intestine.

What is my large intestine?

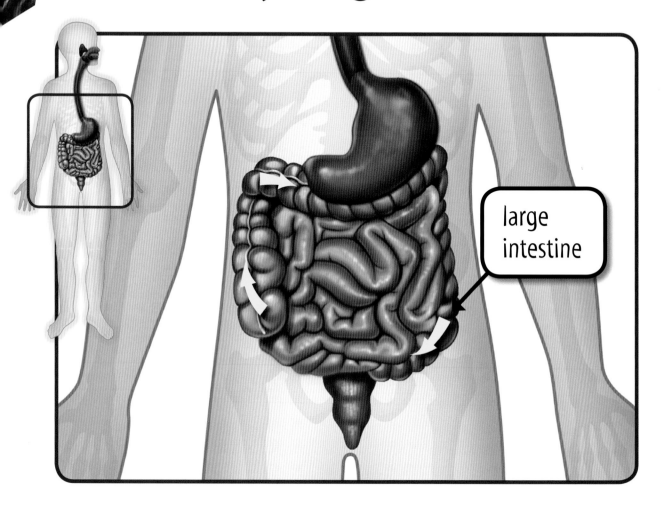

large intestine

Your large intestine is a thick tube that gets rid of food **waste** from the small intestine. Food waste goes into your large intestine. Waste is parts of food your body cannot break down or use.

The waste must be pushed out of your body as **faeces**. If waste stays inside you it will **poison** your body.

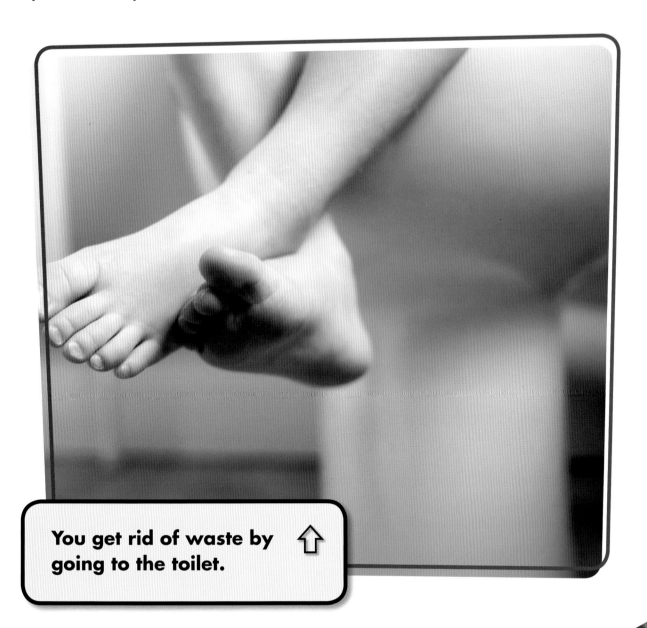

You get rid of waste by going to the toilet. ⬆

What is my liver?

Blood carries **nutrients** from the small intestine to your liver. The liver is an **organ**. An organ is a part of your body that has a certain job to do.

⬆ **You need to eat a mixture of different foods. This means your body will get all the different nutrients it needs to stay healthy.**

Your liver sorts the nutrients and sends them to different parts of your body. Some of them are used to give you **energy**. The liver also stores some nutrients for your body to use later.

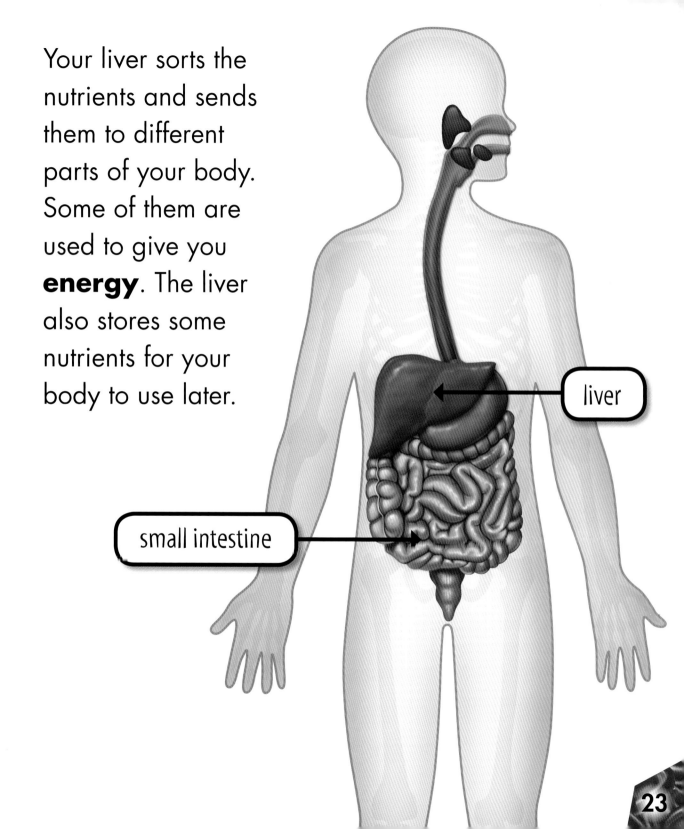

liver

small intestine

What are my kidneys?

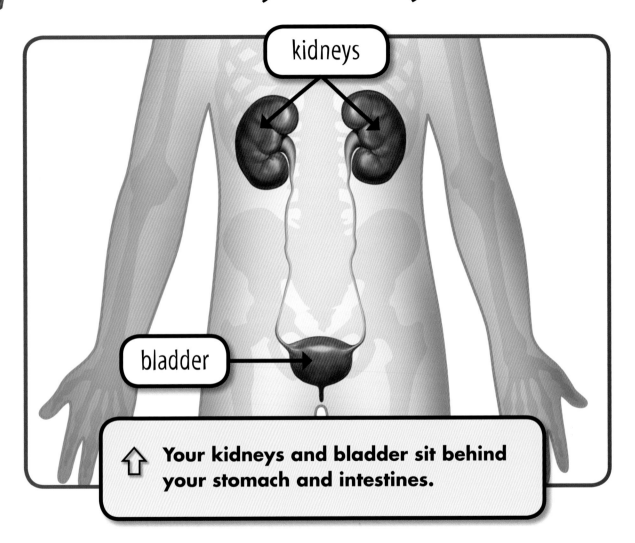

kidneys

bladder

⬆ **Your kidneys and bladder sit behind your stomach and intestines.**

Your kidneys are two small **organs** behind your **stomach**. When your body uses **nutrients** it makes **waste**. Your blood carries the waste to your kidneys.

Your kidneys clean waste materials and water from your blood. The clean blood goes back into the blood system. Waste and spare water go to your **bladder**. They are pushed out of your body as **urine**.

⬆ **You need to drink plenty of water to stay healthy.**

The digestive system

It takes a day or more for food to move through your body. The digestive system works non-stop to give your body everything it needs. It also gets rid of **waste**.

The digestive system

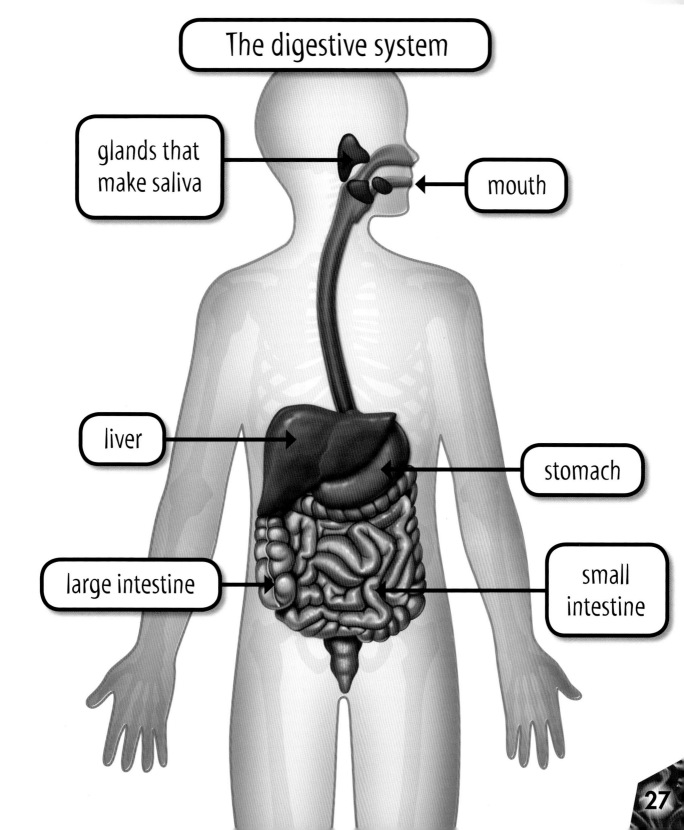

glands that make saliva

mouth

liver

stomach

large intestine

small intestine

What makes me burp?

A burp is made when there is too much air in your **stomach**. If there is too much air, it bubbles up your throat. Then it comes out of your mouth with a burping sound.

Sometimes you swallow air with your food. Gas is also made when food breaks down in your stomach.

Did you know?

It takes about ten seconds for food you swallow to travel to your **stomach**.

The salivary **glands** pump around three cups of saliva into your mouth every day.

The **liquid** food in your stomach is called chyme. The only time you will see chyme is when you are sick!

Your blood passes through your kidneys many times a day.

Your liver makes a liquid called bile. It sends the bile to the small intestine to help break down food.

Glossary

bladder   bag-like organ inside your body. The bladder stores urine before it leaves your body.

digest   break down food into tiny parts so that it can be used by your body

digestive juices   liquids made by glands in your body to help break down food

energy   power used to make things happen. Energy can make things grow, change, or move.

enzyme   substance that speeds actions up in your body. Enzymes can be used to break things down or build things up.

faeces   solid waste that must be pushed out of your body

gland   many glands make enzymes to be used by your body

glucose   simple sugar that your body uses to get energy

liquid   substance, such as water, that can be poured easily

muscle   stretchy part of your body that tightens and relaxes to make movement

nutrient   substance your body needs to live and grow

organ   part of your body that has a certain job to do

poison   substance that can make you ill or even kill you

stomach   organ in your body where food is digested (broken down)

urine   yellowish liquid waste which comes out of your body when you go to the toilet

waste   unwanted material. It is often what is left after useful parts have been taken out.

Find out more

Books to read

Body in Action: Eating by Claire Llewellyn (A&C Black, 2003)

Look After Yourself: Healthy Food by Angela Royston (Heinemann Library, 2003)

My Amazing Body: A First Look at Health and Fitness by Pat Thomas and Lesley Harker (Hodder Wayland, 2002)

My Amazing Body: Eating by Angela Royston (Heinemann Library, 2005)

Websites

http://kidshealth.org/kid/body/digest_SW.html

This website teaches you about the digestive system and how the different parts of the digestive system work. Find out how to keep your digestive system healthy.

http://science.nationalgeographic.com/science/health-and-human-body/human-body/digestive-system-article.html

Click on "feed the system" to see the digestive system working. Try feeding it different foods and see what happens to them.

http://www.welltown.gov.uk/school/dining.html

Find out about the different types of food you need to eat to keep healthy. Learn about food groups. Match different foods to the food groups in a game.

http://www.familyfoodzone.com/kids/main.asp

Fun, interesting games to help you to learn more about food and health.

Index

bile 29
bladder 24–25
burping 28

chyme 29

digestive juices 16
digestive system 5, 8–9, 26–7
drinking 4–5

eating 4–5
energy 4, 6, 23
enzymes 11, 16

faeces 21
food 5, 6, 8, 10–11, 12, 14–19, 26

glands 11, 16, 29
glucose 6

kidneys 24–5, 29

large intestine 20, 27
liquid food 17, 18
liver 9, 22–3, 27

mouth 8, 10–11, 27
muscles 13–15, 17

nutrients 6–7, 19, 22–3, 24

saliva 11, 27, 29
small intestine 18–19, 29
stomach 9, 13–18, 27–29
swallowing 11–13

teeth 10
throat 12–13
tongue 8, 10, 12

urine 25

waste from food 20–1, 24–5, 26